# Dear Malala,
## We Stand with You

Rosemary McCarney with Plan International

CROWN BOOKS
FOR YOUNG READERS
NEW YORK

# Who Is Malala?

On October 9, 2012, a fifteen-year-old girl on her way home from school in Pakistan was shot in the head by a member of the Taliban. Malala Yousafzai had been speaking out in public about the right of all girls to have an education—something the Taliban were against. They thought that shooting her would stop her campaign, but they didn't know how strong Malala is. She was flown to England for lifesaving treatment, and has recovered. Malala and two other girls who were wounded in the attack are attending school and living in England. Malala is more determined than ever to work for every child's right to an education. For her bravery and effort on behalf of all children, she has received almost thirty awards and honors, including Pakistan's National Youth Peace Prize, the KidsRights International Children's Peace Prize, President Clinton's Global Citizen Award, the Ambassador of Conscience Award from Amnesty International, and the Freedom of Thought Prize from the European Parliament. In 2013, Malala Yousafzai became the youngest person ever nominated for the Nobel Peace Prize.

*Peru*

Dear Malala,

*Niger*

We have never met before, but I feel like I know you.

*El Salvador*

I have never seen you before, but I've heard your voice.

*Indonesia*

To girls like me, you are a leader who encourages us.
And you are a friend.

*Nicaragua*

Because of your courage, there are even special days named after you.
Malala Days—all over the world.

*Nepal*

The first time I heard about you was such a terrible day.
You had been shot simply because you went to school. But you survived.

Zimbabwe

You still wanted to learn.
You spoke up for yourself and other girls, too.

*Brazil*

People everywhere wondered why it was so hard for girls to get an education.

*Myanmar*

But you and I know the answer.

*Liberia*

In many countries, bullets are not the only way to silence girls.

Early marriage . . .

*Philippines*

poverty . . .

Cameroon

discrimination . . .

*Indonesia*

violence . . . all play a part.

Kenya

But because you are a girl, you have shown
the world that these things will not stop you.

*India*

You, Malala, have reminded us that it is your right,
my right—*every* child's right—to go to school.

India

Instead of living in fear...

*Kenya*

we must shout for change.

*China*

Because I am a girl, I am writing to
let you know that every day is Malala Day.

Paraguay

Girls everywhere are behind you.

*Nepal*

*Uganda*

We are raising our hands to stand with you
and demand a chance for everyone.

Germany

Niger

We are all Malala.

United States

The world will see what girls can achieve—if only they let us.

*On July 12, 2013, the day of her sixteenth birthday, Malala Yousafzai stood to speak to nearly 1,000 delegates to the United Nations' Youth Assembly. The secretary-general of the UN had just proclaimed that day to be Malala Day. Here are parts of Malala Yousafzai's speech.*

"So here I stand . . . one girl among many. I speak—not for myself, but for all girls and boys. I raise up my voice—not so that I can shout, but so that those without a voice can be heard. Those who have fought for their rights: their right to live in peace; their right to be treated with dignity; their right to equality of opportunity; their right to be educated.

Dear friends, on the ninth of October, 2012, the Taliban shot me on the left side of my forehead. They shot my friends, too. They thought that the bullets would silence us.

But they failed. Weakness, fear, and hopelessness died. Strength, power, and courage were born. I am the same Malala. My ambitions are the same. My hopes are the same. My dreams are the same.

We want schools and education for every child's bright future. We will continue our journey to our destination of peace and education for everyone. No one can stop us. We will speak for our rights and we will bring change through our voice. We must believe in the power and the strength of our words. Our words can change the world. Because we are all together, united for the cause of education. And if we want to achieve our goal, then let us empower ourselves with the weapon of knowledge and let us shield ourselves with unity and togetherness.

Dear brothers and sisters, we must not forget that millions of people are suffering from poverty, injustice, and ignorance. We must not forget that millions of children are out of schools. We must not forget that our sisters and brothers are waiting for a bright, peaceful future.

So let us wage a global struggle against illiteracy, poverty, and terrorism, and let us pick up our books and pens. They are our most powerful weapons.

One child, one teacher, one pen, and one book can change the world.

Education is the only solution. Education first."

# How You Can Help

*(Always ask your parents or teachers before posting
any photographs or personal information on the Internet.)*

## DONATE

Plan International's **Because I am a Girl Fund** focuses on girls' education, with a global initiative to get girls into school for a minimum of nine years of quality education by building schools, training teachers, and advocating for every girl's right to go to school. **plan-international.org/girls**

**The Malala Fund,** inspired by Malala's commitment to advocate for every girl to go to school, empowers girls to reach out and lend a hand to those in need of an education. **malalafund.org**

**Girls Inc.** inspires all girls to be strong, smart, and bold, through delivery of capacity-building programs in schools across North America, to help girls ages six to eighteen navigate gender, economic, and social barriers. **girlsinc.org**

## PARTICIPATE

**#GIRLWITHABOOK** Sparked when UN Secretary-General Ban Ki-moon said, "Nothing is scarier to terrorists than a girl with a book," #GIRLWITHABOOK encourages girls from all over the world to take photos of themselves with a book. Add your photo to the movement on Pinterest: **pinterest.com/lenashareef/girlwithabook**

**#BecauseOfSchool** Tell the world what your education has helped you achieve and share the impact education has had on your life. **globalpartnership.org/becauseofschool**

**Girl Rising** uses the power of storytelling to spread the message that educating girls changes society for the better. Use writing, film, or art to share your personal messages about education with the world. **girlrising.com**

# Acknowledgments

Many hands created this beautiful tribute to a remarkable young woman. The Plan International Communications team was inspired by the United Nations' declaring July 12, 2013, Malala Day, when 500 young people "took over" the UN for the first time, with the ready support of the UN secretary-general. They produced a short film depicting girls from all over the world writing to Malala to tell her how important a symbol she was for them in their lives. Jen Albaugh helped me turn the warm and powerful video into this book, choosing the incredible photographs Plan has collected from around the world to bring the girls' words to life. Malala's charm, courage, and conviction are an inspiration to all of them and to all of us. Heartfelt thanks to everyone on the Plan teams who helped me bring this story to life.

—Rosemary McCarney

Text copyright © 2014 by Plan Canada
Front cover photograph copyright © 2013 by Gretel Truong/
A World at School; back cover photographs copyright
© 2013 by Shona Hamilton/Plan (top left), Gretel Truong/A World
at School (bottom left), and Shreeram KC/Plan (right)

Visit us on the Web! randomhousekids.com

Educators and librarians, for a variety of teaching tools,
visit us at RHTeachersLibrarians.com

Library of Congress Cataloging-in-Publication Data
is available upon request.
ISBN 978-0-553-52120-7 (trade)
ISBN 978-0-553-52121-4 (lib. bdg.)
ISBN 978-0-553-52122-1 (ebook)

Printed in the United States of America
10 9 8 7 6 5 4 3 2 1
First Crown Edition 2015

This book is dedicated to
the 65 million girls in
the world today who are
in neither primary school
nor secondary school.

## PHOTOGRAPH CREDITS

Alf Berg/Plan: 13; Will Boase/Plan: 24 (right);
Niels Busch/Plan: 18, 19; Campaign to End Child
Marriage Netherlands/Plan: 14; Ruth Catsburg/Plan:
11; Floor Catshoek/Plan: 7; Catherine Farquharson/
Plan: 20; Shona Hamilton/Plan: 5, 6, 25 (right);
Shreeram KC/Plan: 9, 24 (left); Connelly La Mar/
Plan: 22; Alexandra Kensland Letelier/Plan: 26;
Annie Mpalume/Plan: 10; Rebecca Nduku/Plan:
21; Dyayi Nuswantari P./Plan: 17; Plan/Plan: 8;
Friedrun Reinhold/Plan: 25 (left); Daniel Silva/Plan:
4; Warisara Sornpet/Plan: 12, 15; Lucas Sosa/Plan:
23; James Stone/Plan: 16; Gretel Truong/A World at
School: 2; Gary Walker/Plan: 31.